UNION
with
GOD

Library of Spiritual Classics

Union with God makes the third book we have published in the Spiritual Classics series. We began this series—and this publishing company—with the book *Practicing His Presence*. We were not at all sure the idea of digging up the great spiritual classics of the past (which were generally either out of print or almost unreadable) would find an audience large enough to even defer the printing costs. Happily such an audience was there.

Our next book will be *The Spiritual Guide* by Michael Molinos. Without doubt this book has the most dramatic history of any piece of Christian literature. You will find it in every way a classic on the subject of the deeper Christian life.

We sincerely appreciate hearing from you about our books and what part they have played in your life.

Jeanne Guyon

UNION
with
GOD

The SeedSowers

Union With God

First printing August 1981
Second printing January 1999

Published by   SeedSowers Publishing
                  P.O. Box 3317, Jacksonville, FL 32206
                  1-800-228-2665

Library of Congress Cataloging-in-Publication Data

Guyon, Jeanne
        Union With God / Jeanne Guyon
        ISBN 10digit: 0-940232-057
        ISBN 13 digit: 978-0-940232-05-1
        1. Spiritual Life   1. Title

Time New Roman 12pt

Contents

Union With God ———————————

Acknowledgment

The most famous works of Jeanne Guyon are her *Autobiography* and *Experiencing the Depths of Jesus Christ.* This book, *Union with God*, should also be included because of its content and practical help. The probable reason that this book is less known than the other two is that it was the most obscure, vague and difficult book to read of all the books Guyon penned. In the Epilogue of *Experiencing the Depths of Jesus Christ* I quoted a passage from the original translation which should remove all question concerning the enormous difficulty faced in trying to understand this book.

On several occasions I have attempted to rewrite this book in modern English but abandoned the task. How could I edit what I could not comprehend? I was pleasantly surprised—perhaps amazed is a better word—when my wife, Helen, placed a complete and lucid rewrite of this book in my hands. It is, then, to a woman that we owe the original authenticity of *Union with God*, and to a woman we owe the reclamation and resurrection of this book.

It is to Carman, Annie and Joannie we owe our gratitude for the mundane tasks of typing and typesetting this book. The cover comes to us through the joint efforts of two men of art, Michelangelo and Brad.

Introduction

Union with God belongs to a trilogy.* Jeanne Guyon authored many books, but her greater influence, practical help and historical contribution lie in three books and her letters and poems.

As you read *Union with God* you will see Jeanne Guyon taking you through progressive stages that carry one from conversion to a state the Roman Catholics referred to as union with the Lord. This progression toward God through certain plateaus was the traditional Catholic way of seeing spiritual matters. For Roman Catholics this approach is rooted in strong historical precedent.

In the fifth century a Catholic monk living somewhere in Syria wrote on stages of spirituality, beginning with conversion and going on to something he referred to as divine union. From that time forward, for Catholics, the most acceptable way to express their view on spiritual growth was by writing—or speaking—of progressive stages. Writers' views might vary on what the stages were, but placing their views

---

* The other two books are *Experiencing the Depths of Jesus Christ* and *Madame Guyon's Autobiography.*

within the context of this progression was almost a necessity if they were to be considered orthodox. It was in the 1200-year-old mold that Jeanne Guyon cast this book. What you actually have here, though, is Jeanne Guyon's own spiritual pilgrimage as she understood and interpreted it. Certainly she never intended the progressive stages she presents here as the only way to know the Lord deeply. Personally I doubt that there is any set progression in the deeper Christian life, as we have a Lord of infinite variety who provides each of us the opportunity of a unique spiritual history.

Guyon herself makes a unique presentation in this book in that she unfolds a more scripturally founded view than did her predecessors, who were more Platonic than Christian in their teachings.

One other point needs to be made that has to do with the historical influence of this particular book. From time to time a group of Christians will arise who teach the novel idea that it is possible to stop sinning. As a proof text they will sometimes quote this book. No less a man than John Wesley theorized it was possible to live a sinless life, but fortunately never claimed such a state for himself. Neither did Guyon. (Proponents of sinless perfection have always had to deal with one major problem: They have never come up with a person who was generally accepted to be perfect. In recent years the idea has, mercifully, virtually disappeared as a serious subject of consideration.) I only hope no modern reader will interpret Jeanne Guyon's use of the word "perfect" (by which she meant the human will in concert with the divine will) as a reference to a state of sinlessness.

With those two observations made we send this book forth into the Christian community to bless, encourage and strengthen.

Gene Edwards
Quebec City
Canada

Union With God —————————————

1

Your way to God begins on the day of your conversion, for conversion marks your soul's initial return to God. From that moment you begin to live and have your being by the means of His grace. After your conversion, your own *spirit*—the human spirit (which is deep within your inmost being)—is touched by God and is made alive and functioning. Your spirit—in turn—invites your *soul* to compose itself and to turn within, there to find the God who has newly come to reside at the center of your being. Your spirit instructs your soul that, since God is more present deep within you, He *cannot* be found anywhere else. Henceforth, He *must* be sought within. And He must be enjoyed there alone.

Therefore, from the very beginning you find great joy in knowing that your Lord is within you and that you can find Him and enjoy Him in your inmost being. From the very beginning of your conversion, from the

very outset of your life in Christ, it is possible for you
to know that what you are to pursue is that inward life.

*From that turn unto Him whom the Children
of Israel have so deeply revolted.*
                                        (Isaiah 31:6)

What is conversion? It is nothing more than turning
from your created nature and *returning* to God who now
resides at the center of your being. Your conversion is
not just a matter of turning from sin. Turning from sin
to grace is certainly essential in salvation but is not *all*
that salvation involves. For it to be complete,
conversion is not only a turning from outward things
but a turning to the inmost portions of your being—to
that place where the Lord has come to reside.

When you are thus turned toward God, you find it
easy to return there again and again. The longer you
continue to turn inward to God, the *nearer* you are
drawn to Him and the more firmly you adhere to Him.
Consequently, you are further removed from your more
outward and natural man, which is so often contrary to
God. By moving into that inmost sanctuary again and
again, you will finally become so established in your
conversion that it becomes natural, even habitual, to
live in the presence of God. And where is God's
presence? God's presence is where He lodges. . .deep
in your spirit.

Now do not suppose that such a state is reached by exertion or by effort on *your* part. The only thing which you yourself are capable of doing is this: to withdraw from external objects. In other words, the most you can do is turn inward. Yes, you are capable of that much. You are capable of cooperating with divine grace to that extent; therefore, you should attempt to do so. Beyond that, you have only to continue to be firm in adhering to the God who is within you.

Your Lord has a virtue of magnetic attraction. He draws you more and more powerfully to Himself. As He attracts you inwardly, He purifies you of all the things that are not of Himself. But remember, this is *His* activity, not *yours*. Just as it is with impure vapor, so it is with you. Vapor is drawn up by the sun and as it gradually ascends, it is rarified and made pure. The vapor's only contribution to this process is to remain passive and rise. In our experience, there is a slight difference from that of the vapor. You and I have the privilege of cooperating voluntarily with the Lord's drawing of us toward Him. This inward turning to Him is very easy, natural, and effortless because He is at your center. Your turning is because He is drawing you.

There is a principle in nature: The center of anything exerts a powerful drawing force. This principle is just as true in the spiritual realm as in nature—even more so, for it is a more exalted realm of existence. The drawing of the force that is within your center is even more irresistible than that which is found in nature.

In the natural realm there is the magnetic attraction toward the center. In every creature there is a strong tendency to be reunited with its center, but in the spiritual realm this tendency is vigorous and active in proportion to the spiritual level of the person involved.

As soon as anything turns inward toward the center, then that thing begins picking up extensive momentum and will progress toward its center very rapidly. The only real exception to this occurs if it so happens that an obstacle is in the way.

If you hold a stone in your hand, it is no sooner let go than it begins to fall by its own weight back to its true center, the earth. The same is true also with water. Water will flow without hesitation towards its center. Such a thing is always true unless there is a barrier or obstruction in the way.

The same is true of your soul. When your soul has been converted, it attempts to turn back to its God. When your soul turns within to reunite with the Lord who is within, your soul is under the influence of this same law of central tendencies. The soul falls gradually to its proper center without any other force than the precious weight of love. The more tranquil the soul remains, the more it is freed from an effort to propel its own self. The tranquil soul does not try to get to the center by its efforts. The more rapidly and unobstructed the soul advances toward the center, the more the center has full liberty to draw the soul.

It is obvious, then, that you should give all your attention toward turning inward to the place of your Lord's residence. Do not be discouraged by the fact that you might find this a difficult exercise in the beginning. Before very long, an abundant grace will come to you and this matter will become easy. That is true *if* you are faithful in meekly withdrawing your heart from outward distractions and occupations and then returning to your center with affections full of tenderness and serenity.

Now, when your emotions and feelings are turbulent with anxiety and anger, then be assured that a general retreat inward to the presence of God deadens these turbulent emotions. If you try any other way of opposing these emotions and feelings, you will succeed only in irritating them—not stilling them.

Knowing that, your purpose is to pursue the inward life. This is the spring of all the joy of the soul. This is the solid foundation of all spiritual progress. Your purpose is to pursue that life which dwells deep within your inmost center.

If you turn toward God merely by your intelligence, you may enjoy some spiritual contemplation, but you will never enter into an intimate union with God unless, of course, you quit your way and enter into this higher way of the inward touch. All working is in the spirit.

On the other hand, if you are led by a Lord who is deep within your spirit, you will be conducted by a blind abandonment and not by intelligence. You will experience a certain kind of knowledge but it will be a knowledge that is delightful and fruitful. You would not be walking by your intellect. If you seek the Lord by intellectual enjoyment, you receive a very distinct light to guide you. Not so the one who walks by blind abandonment. He has no clear view of the road. If you know God primarily by the light of your intellect, you will never enter those imperceptible passes of the spirit which are reserved for the abandoned soul alone. If you seek God by your intellect, you will move with a sure step. Why? You will proceed with the evidence furnished through an illumination that is assisted by the strengths of reasoning.

Not so the simple believer. You must be led in the inward way. You are destined to pursue blindly an unknown course which, though it seems perfectly natural to you, requires you to sense your way along by that intuitive life which dwells deep within you and which draws you forward. In spite of this seeming uncertainty of your way, as a simple and trusting believer you will make progress in spirit with *far more certainty* than you will as an intellectual believer! As contradictory as it seems, intellectual illuminations are subject to misleadings; yes, far more severe than those of the inward way. When you are abandoned into that unknown course you will be guided by a supreme will which conducts you wherever *He* desires. You will follow a path prescribed for you by a touch of God from deep within your spirit. You will pursue a way of faith and absolute abandonment and will have neither liberty nor desire for any other path. As you grow accustomed to this way, any other way will become burdensome and even embarrassing to you.

True, the way of faith is not as self-gratifying nor as exciting as the way of intellectual illumination. In fact, the way of faith is sometimes very dry. Your thoughts wander far more and have nothing to fix them.

Please recognize that there are great differences in people. For instance, some people are more sensitive to pleasures than others. It is the same way with those who are led by the spirit. Some believers have a great deal of emotion or enthusiasm. But they may, nonetheless, acquire no more than someone else of that which is truly the Lord deep within. Such a person should restrain his outer disposition and allow these emotions to pass. That would be true even when those emotions seem to be burning with love for the Lord. Yet another believer might seem harder and more insensible to the things of Christ, giving the appearance of being altogether in the natural man; but sometimes there is a delicate something in the depths of the spirit of that person which serves to nourish him. True, his encounter with the Lord may be in a much more condensed form; nonetheless, he shares in an acquaintance with God which is just as real (or perhaps even more so) than the other believer who is so full of zeal or ardor.

Now I must point out to you that those who are led most delicately by the indwelling spirit are also those who suffer greatly. In times of testing and tribulation, these believers suffer more than others do. Such a believer's delicate spirit is sometimes almost imperceptible during times of great trouble. His emotions are delicate and concealed. His spirit, therefore, tends to have the same characteristics. We can say of such a Christian that he does not have a strongly motivated spirit but a delicate one. He is more indifferent, more insensible, and yet we must say he is more stable. Nonetheless, be clear in knowing that such a person's problems come to him just the same as all others. Though he may not do things impulsively, he nonetheless does the same things just as much in his natural man as does the enthusiast. His problem is that he cannot find that feeble, sensitive moving of a hidden spirit. Thus unequipped, he cannot make headway against his foes. (Nonetheless, such a believer is often characterized by a greater loyalty than others. I would have you to note the striking difference between Peter and John. One seemed to be overflowing with extraordinary zeal but fell away at the voice of a young girl. The other, John, seemed to have no external manifestations of those things which were going on within him; nonetheless, he remained faithful to the very end.)

Perhaps, then, you would like to ask: If a person is urged on by no strong guidance, but walks blindly, is such a person really a follower of God? My answer is yes. That person does God's will even more truly than the one filled with sight. True, he may not have the satisfaction of knowing that he is doing the will of God; nonetheless, the Lord's will is engraved in indelible letters on his innermost parts. He therefore performs in firm and indestructible abandonment. He goes steadily under the influence of God's touch and the influence of his spirit; he progresses from one degree to another by faith. True, it is a faith which is manifested more at some times than it is at other times, as he alternates between a sense of dryness and a sense of the presence of God. His enjoyment of the Lord, nonetheless becomes continually deeper. Paradoxically, as the enjoyment of the Lord deepens, it also becomes less perceptible. As his enjoyment of the Lord becomes less perceptible, his sense of the Lord becomes more inward—even more delicate than ever before. For a Christian such as this, even in the midst of dryness he is delighted. His delight is *not* coming by distinct nor intellectual illumination. Though his soul is not aware of the light that he is receiving, it receives all the benefits of that light! This is so true that this believer finds himself more acquainted with the truth (I mean that truth implanted in his inmost being). This acquaintance he has causes everything in him to yield to the will of God. As a result, God's will gradually grows more familiar to him. Eventually, he is more able, in this very weak and imperceptible way, to penetrate a thousand mysteries—mysteries which he could never have discovered by light of reason or knowledge! He is gradually preparing, without even being aware of it, for even greater levels of progress which lie out there before him.

The trials which you might expect to encounter at this point in your spiritual growth are trials of alternating dryness and enjoyment. The dry times serve to purify that mixture of self which often enters and pollutes a pure enjoyment of the Lord. (If this did not happen to you, your emotions and natural desires would attach themselves to your enjoyment of God within. This is a state less than the purity which the Lord is after in His relationship to you.)

As you make your pilgrimage through this level of spiritual progress, therefore, you may expect to encounter these alternating times of enjoyment, then dryness, and *then* true progress. You may have no great testings except, perhaps, some transitory passing problems such as dealing with certain faults of your own personality. But remember that at every level of spiritual progress, your natural faults are much more likely to overtake you in *dry* times than in seasons of inner joy. At times of inner joy, the anointing of His grace protects you from a thousand evils.

In the beginning of your pilgrimage, when God first turned your soul to look inward, He so influenced your soul against itself that your soul cut off all its other enjoyments, even the most innocent ones. Sometimes, during this period, the soul begins to loathe itself. The soul finds no release in self-loathing until the natural senses and appetites (and the likes and dislikes) of the soul are completely destroyed. Many Christians, it seems, seek to overcome their former habits by all sorts of painful self-denial. But, the true destruction of the former likes and dislikes of natural man are best taken care of when the inward drawing is vigorous and the anointing within is very active. Your Lord will uncover everything the soul contrives to cover. He does this uncovering so that He can enable you to conquer and overcome the natural tendencies of your soul.

And what is the eventual outcome when you choose *this* course in dealing with the external problem of the Christian's life? A constant practice of turning inward, there touching the Lord's gracious anointing. With this touch He draws you to Himself. Eventually, His Life and Spirit—dwelling deep within you—get the upper hand of your external nature. After all, your natural man is an inferior part of you. The Lord, who dwells supreme in the innermost portions of your being, is the higher portion of you. This inferior portion, this natural man, comes under subjection. Without resistance, without striving and without struggle, the external weaknesses are cared for.

When a Christian has arrived at a place where he is no longer greatly affected by periods of dryness, you might make an error in believing that he has come to something of a state of the death of the natural man. In a sense, one might say it is death, but *only* to worrisome and superficial emotions. But such a state is a long way from the death of *self* and from a complete union with God in his spirit.

Union With God ——————

2

As you look back on the last chapter, you may conclude that at this point your soul will have reached its proper state. The soul is silent before God, is constantly breathing out love and is, therefore, the instrument of the most powerful amorous activity. You are responding to divine love which is being extended to you by Him. Furthermore, your soul is even leaping constantly toward this divine love. In this interaction of activity, there is oftentimes an accompanying light and an almost constant sense of peace. I must add, though, that it is also from this interacting of love that you may come not only to practice some of the greatest virtues, but also some of the most severe self-denials.

We have seen that you are best rid of distractions by being drawn inwardly to the Lord and not by wrestling with them. As you enjoy the time of victory over outward distractions, you may begin to believe that you are forever free from an enemy whose power has been destroyed. You may feel you have paid a high price for the ground you have gained. You may be very surprised, therefore, when you come upon a dry spell. This dry spell will serve to remind you, in a very striking manner, that you have other outward weaknesses.

When you have entered into that time of your life when your soul sits quietly and lovingly before the Lord, you can be very surprised to suddenly find a dry spell in your life. Not only has a dry spell emerged along with the discovery of previously unseen faults, but even old ones begin reappearing. Looking about you, you may feel that your former strength for doing battle is drying up.

Why is this taking place? To the exact proportion that your self-effort is laid aside, so also your strength for resisting diminishes. As you continue to advance toward the Lord, so the power of your soul becomes less active and you become, paradoxically, weak in combat. In other words, as God becomes stronger within you, so you become weaker.

At first sight, this seems to be a very dangerous condition for a Christian to find himself in. But do not fail to recognize *this* fact: All your labors, even when aided by grace, cannot accomplish the conquest of those outward things which distract your life. If you *were* strong, you still could not conquer the weakness of your outer life. Under no circumstance are you able to effectively deal with such things. It is the Lord Himself who takes gradual possession of your soul. It is He, and He alone, who becomes your purifier.

In the beginning, He required you to be very watchful. Then He led you into a deep relationship of love. Beyond this point is His requirement that you remain steadfast and let Him do all the work. Watch as He will begin to manifest Himself to you as Lord of all things. See *Him* as He subjects the flesh to the spirit! All true *outward* improvement comes only after *inward* development. Outward improvement is totally dependent upon the inward.

When you are engaged in action and devotion, however simple they may be, you are also putting into action some outward, undesirable habits of the soul.

Therefore, turn inward.

Up until now you have witnessed the destruction of many things that belong to *outward* senses. *Now*, there are inward activities of the soul which must also be defeated. How is this done? Such is brought about by a delightful resting and a ceasing of working, while your Lord, in turn, works deep within you.

Do not be surprised if, during this time, God seems to be neglecting His work on your outer man. This is why these outward defects which you thought had been destroyed have reappeared!

You have arrived at a new place in your journey toward the Lord. You can expect your dry spells to be longer and more frequent, and the longer and dryer these times are, the greater will be your weaknesses. Such things have fallen to you so that your soul's relationship to the spirit is more purified and, therefore, more *trustable*. The dryness and weakness which purify your soul's activities and the love relationship that is going on between your soul and the indwelling Lord work together to put an end to things external.

You will notice that until now, the Christian's experience alternates between enjoyment and dryness. Dryness will always purify the joy. And the joy that follows the dryness? It, too, will be purified by the *next* encounter of dryness. This process is always painful to a believer. As a result, he feels quite weak and barren.

As soon as you become sufficiently weak that you cease fashioning *your own* concept of self-denial, then your Lord will come, take over, and accomplish the defeat of the flesh more thoroughly than you could ever do! And how does He do this? By dispensing the cross to you according to your measure. The cross you encounter is not a cross which you will choose but a cross which you receive by His sovereignty over your life.

3

As you move more toward the center, you must at some point arrive at a state of naked faith. You will come to naked faith as a natural result of what has happened to you. All things else, both outward and inward, are desolation.

What am I saying?

We have seen a forward progress in your spiritual growth and we see that progress taking many years. Yet, at some point, this progress—acquired at such cost—*must be taken away.* Whether suddenly or gradually, *all* the progress made is lost. With that, you will begin perhaps the longest stage of your journey. Surely, this may not appear to be a happy state, but at its end is a death of your self-nature. (I qualify that: a death of the self-nature *if* you are willing to consent to be left in such desolation.) This is a desolation so long and so complete that the soul finally dies to self.

There are an infinite number of Christians who

never pass the earlier stages in their movement toward a deep union with the Lord. Consequently, those who *reach* this particular plateau are very few; and those who *complete* this particular portion of the sojourn are fewer still.

This desolation—or total desertedness—comes as a sudden and violent occurrence for many believers who encounter this experience. I will speak momentarily of those upon whom this state arrives slowly. But if their introduction is sudden and violent, they really have less reason to complain. The very severity of such a sudden affliction serves as a kind of consolation. You see, there are others who come upon this experience as something enfeebling. The end result of this experience for them is a disgust for everything. Thus, they *appear* to have an unwillingness to obey the Lord.

Now let us consider this time of desolation. You will be first deprived of the works which you formerly accomplished voluntarily; that is, you become unable to do what you could formerly do very easily. As this desolation increases, you will begin to feel a general inability in all things. This state does not get better, but rather enlarges day after day. This weakness and inability take complete possession until finally you say:

> *That which I do, I do not wish to do. But what*
> *I would do, I will not. What I hate, that is*
> *what I do.* (Rom. 7:15)

After you have been deprived of all past progress—both inward progress and outward progress (all of which might be referred to as *non*essential)—the Lord begins to work on those things which *are* essential. Every Christian virtue—even the ones that you have taken for granted—disappear*. As they depart, you lose all joy within; there is a sense of inward loss. I would like to point out that this is not a real loss in your spirit. The loss is only in your consciousness. You can be sure that your spirit is still strong. But from *your* viewpoint, there seems to be no apparent activity deep within you. The presence of your spirit is imperceptible to you. And the Lord who is there in your spirit is also imperceptible to you.

Please know, it is *necessary* that the reality of your spirit be hidden. If it were not, the death and the loss of self could not be accomplished. The spirit retires within. The spirit is shut up so closely that you are not even aware that your spirit exists.

You will ask yourself again and again, *Why has this desolation come upon me and why was it necessary?* The whole object of this journey, thus far, has been to take you first from outward ways to a singleness of

---

* *Editor's Note: It is not likely that anyone who has read this book so far would suppose that Madame Guyon's reference to "every Christian virtue disappears" is a reference to the person being allowed to fall into open sin. These Christian virtues simply disappear only from his own eyes. To others, as well as to God, he exhibits, as ever, the Lord Jesus Christ.*

heart; then second, to sensing the realm of the spirit within you; and third, to an awareness of the loss of the sense of the presence of your spirit. Finally, there comes a painful awareness of the loss of everything.

Perhaps it could be stated differently. The course begins vigorously in the realm of the seen. This *seeing the seen* and *not* seeing the unseen is a state every believer begins in, regardless of the singleness of his heart. Next, you leave the realm of the seen and are introduced to unseen, spiritual realms where we live by faith and are nourished by love. Later, you leave that spiritual level and enter into naked faith. Here you are left dead to all spiritual experiences. It is at this juncture in your life that you die to yourself. Having then died to yourself, you pass into God. It is from this point on that one lives from the life of God alone.

Can you see the progression? In the beginning, God dispenses His grace to you in such a way that you begin with things of the outward senses; then you advance toward things that are spiritual. You end by what seems to be a leaving even of this realm. Finally, your inner man is brought gradually to its center and united wholly with God.

The more deeply your soul retires into the most hidden parts of your being, the more you are knit into *singleness*; that is, you cannot continue to scatter yourself among a thousand things at this point. You have lost not only the ability to accomplish all those myriads of things, you have also lost the ability to be keenly conscious of them. You are entirely stripped, and gradually you lose not only everything but you also lose yourself. (Either that or you are forced to desert the things of self because your inward desolation has caused you to lose the ability to even be aware of the things of yourself.)

You now find yourself stripped, without mercy, of everything within and without. You seem to have lost all that meant anything to your outward nature and all that was of any value to your *inward* nature. What a seemingly unchristian state for a Christian to be in. Nonetheless, the pilgrimage is by no means at its (*seemingly*) lowest point.

Next, and this is the portion of the pilgrimage that has the appearance of being the worst of all, you are delivered over to temptations—or perhaps we should say testings. The more you are tempted, the more you seem to be deprived of all strength to resist external things. You are at a time when you are at your weakest and you are subject to all sorts of attacks. It is in *this* precarious hour that the strength of your spirit is removed from you! In the removing of this last place of refuge, all evidence of the goodness of God seems to depart with it. You have lost the faithfulness of God. You have lost the faithfulness of your spirit. . . faithfulness to its very own nature.

Now what do we see here before us? We see you, a devotee of Christ, stripped of all the things you so desperately need in order to deal with a powerful enemy in hard pursuit.

You go on fighting and defending yourself as well as you possibly can, watching for every opportunity to discover a stronghold of safety. But the longer you fight, the weaker you become. Your enemy, in turn, is constantly increasing in strength.

What then shall you do? Obviously, you must get to the gate of your fortress as quickly as you can and find aid there, abundant aid, if at all possible. But alas, you reach your fortress and find it closed. And rather than giving you any aid, the keeper has barricaded every possible door to refuge. You fall into the hands of your powerful enemy. But miracle of miracles, when you are defenseless, in complete despair, and have utterly given up, you recognize your enemy as your best and truest friend!

You can be sure, if you come this far in this pilgrimage, *you* will touch upon all the experiences described herein. Perhaps they will manifest themselves in ways totally unlike the description given here. But *this* experience, essentially, somehow awaits you: the loss of every blessing, the development of all sorts of weaknesses, the powerlessness to protect yourself, no rest or sanctuary in your spirit, God Himself seeming to be angry, and—to crown it all—you find temptations on every hand.

I think I hear you say, *I would willingly endure all that if I could be sure, in that hour, that my will was in harmony with God's will and I could know that I was not following my fallen nature.*

Ah! Of course you would! You would also be *happy*! But such cannot be. As you become weak and lose your ability even to love, your spirit also becomes weak. You see, your spirit has been nourished by the strength of your love for the Lord. . .and by His love for you. But now your very spirit seems to have vanished! Your spirit is not manifesting itself anywhere, by *any* sign. Certainly your spirit is not taking part in anything that is happening to you. The conclusion, then, is that your spirit is separating itself from you and is furnishing you no strength. Consequently, you feel that you are living completely by your own strength, your own will, and are consenting to your natural man. Because you cannot sense your spirit, your own will is all that you are aware of.

You will recall that in an earlier chapter I said that in your journey toward union with the Lord, the natural senses are subdued and extinguished. This is true. But why this occurrence? Because of the earlier victories which grace has granted you. Because of these, however, you become high-minded! Nothing can prevent that, really. The soul, sometimes unconsciously, clings tightly to its own elevated opinion of what is good. So, while you stand there believing that the baser things of your nature are dead, God seemingly resurrects your fleshly nature in order to use it as an instrument to expose the exalted position of your soul! He is determined to subdue not only your flesh, but also your soul, in its totality.

Dear Christian, do not fear that by the Lord's (seeming) resurrecting of your fleshly nature, He will allow you to fall into gross sins. No, He has already extracted the venom from the viper! Otherwise, He would not make use of it! At this present level of your spiritual sojourn, the Lord can·safely employ your baser nature because He has already extracted that evil force which, in former times, has been so violent and so criminal. He now takes your baser nature and uses it as an antidote on an exalted soul!

If you can see the grace and wisdom of God's ways in bringing a believer to the total death of self, then you will be filled with delight at His seemingly unusual ways. Even though you may not sense everything outwardly or inwardly, yet you will be overcome with love.

(These little traces of God's grace, when revealed to my heart, have often overwhelmed me with ecstasy.)

Now, if you are going to be faithful to the growth of the Lord's life which is planted within you, you must allow your life to be spoiled, wrecked, and even destroyed to the full extent that God desires it to be, and not be anxious about yourself. Rather, sacrifice to God all your interests—those of time, those of eternity. Do not allow any excuse on your part to retain the slightest atom—for the least little reservation will cause irreparable loss; such reservation prevents the death of self from being total.

You must let God work until He is absolutely satisfied. Let the winds, even the tempests, beat upon you from every direction. You must allow such things, even if you are completely submerged (as we often are), beneath the tumultuous billows that blow.

And now a wonderful thing appears. Far from being estranged from God by your suffering and by the wretchedness of your state . . . your Lord suddenly appears! If He sees any danger of your becoming too weak, He gives you some token of his nearness. He comes as if to assure you, perhaps for only a moment, that He was actually with you throughout all your tribulations. I emphasize the words, *for a moment*, because His revealing Himself in this way is of no permanent value. His appearance is only intended to keep you on the course and to invite you to suffer a further loss of self.

May these words serve to remind you that all the stages we have spoken of are not continuous in violence. There are intermissions, dear Christian. Nonetheless, these moments of respite make the trials, which are sure to return, seem even more painful than before. You see, during the recesses from God's dealing, your soul takes hope—believing perhaps it can escape. Natural things will take every little opportunity to try to save natural life. A drowning man will grab even the blade of a razor. In that frantic moment, he does not think about the pain that will result from his action, he only sees that there is something out there for which he can grasp.

4

Your self-life has now been attacked on all sides by so many enemies. Finally, you have nothing you can do. . .except faint into the arms of love. You have *no other place* to which you can retreat. You see, when death has come and when death has completed its work, the most terrible conditions that could ever exist can cause no further pain or trouble.

And how can you recognize death? Do not think that you will be able to identify the workings of death within the internal parts of your own being. Certainly do not expect to identify the fact that you have passed through the stages that we have discussed here. Death is recognized by that which is absent. It is the inability to feel pain or to have any care or any thought of self. Death is recognized by a permanent indifference. . .and by remaining in that state of indifference forever. . .and *that* without registering even the slightest protest.

Life is evidenced by having a will. . .a will that is *for* something or *against* something. When you have been touched by death, there are no such things. All things will be alike and the same to you. The person touched by death remains dead, no matter what is present before it. Death is an insensitive state, insensitive to everything that concerns itself. Let God reduce you to any extremity, you will know no distaste.

At this point, the Lord will have put all spiritual enemies under His footstool. . .as pertains to your life. Now *He* reigns supreme. He takes you and possesses you more fully, simply because you have completely deserted the self-nature.

I must remind you: These things take place quite slowly and by degrees. (Even after death, this principle remains true. All organisms, even after death, hold some warmth; this is dissipated very gradually.) In fact, in every stage since your conversion and mine there has been a gradual, continual work of cleansing and purifying the soul.

Now that work begins to draw to a completion.

The death of your self-nature does not happen once for all. That will come only in your physical death. You and I vibrate between life and death, being sometimes in one and sometimes in the other.

Finally death is conquered by life. This is the

principle of the resurrection. There is an alternating between life and death until life has finally overcome death.

I have said that this is a slow process, yet it has an element of suddenness about it, too. A believer who is dead finds himself living and he can never doubt he was dead and is now alive again.

(I must point out to you that this death and this resurrection are not yet well established in your life. I would say, instead, it is more like a tendency toward being alive rather than an established and settled experience.)

After your very first experience of grace, which was more or less an outward thing, you turned to the Lord within and began sinking continually toward your center. At the end of this pilgrimage, your soul—lost deep within your spirit—is caused to be enveloped in the arms of Love.

Every person who comes this far has the same experience but each in a different way. The life that has enveloped the soul now arises from within and strongly manifests itself. I would liken this to a living germ which has always existed but has gone unnoticed. Now life causes you to sense the reality of its presence. You realize that life has never been wholly absent, no matter how hidden its presence was.

The dark night that you have gone through is beginning to disappear. The spirit was there, the Lord was there all along; yes, present even in the midst of death. Still, this death was no less death because life was present. The life was concealed in the depths of the death.

A silkworm lies long dead in a cocoon, yet a germ of life is still contained within, awaiting its resurrection. So also in this scope your new life buds, coming forth from out of the innermost center, and from there it begins to grow. Gradually its life extends over your faculties and senses, impregnating each one of them with its own life, and with its natural fruitfulness. Saturated with this new life, you now experience contentment beyond measure. In the strictest sense, it is not your own contentment (nor a contentment *in* the soul), for it is a contentment in God.

I would say that this last statement is especially true for a believer who has advanced far into the state of resurrected life.

I would like to point out that there are some believers who do not pass through this painful death. They only experience a loss of strength and a loss of life; this loss seems to annihilate the central self and causes the believer to die to everything. Here, as in the other case, death is recognized by the total and permanent inability to feel pain or to have any likes or dislikes. Such stages are death *only* to the extent that the person is not experiencing any life. Such a state is not a total death.

We sometimes refer to death as *departure*. We mean there is separation. This is the way I propose to use the term *death*. Death is a separation, a taking leave of the self-nature in order that you may pass into God. *This* state is characterized by a total and entire loss of your will, so that you may exist in God alone.

When I speak of your will, I would like to include even the very best of that which is the will of man. Your will is still very much part of your self-nature, however good and however honorable. These, too, must be destroyed that the will of God alone may remain. Everything born of the will of the flesh, everything that comes out of even your *good* will needs to be brought into complete death. When this happens, nothing but the will of God will be left. When your old will has been completely extinguished, then God's will begins to take its place. Gradually, the Lord's will can change your human will into faith itself!

Does this mean that all your suffering will be past? The self-nature will have expired and entered into an experience with death; there will be *no* obstacle to your being in perfect union with God; yet, for all of this, the inner man has still not passed into God.

That fact is the cause of extreme suffering. So, you see, suffering remains.

I realize that you will object to the above statement. If the self-nature is dead, then how can it suffer?

Your self-nature becomes experientially dead as soon as you are completely separated from it. But this death is not really complete until the inner man has passed into God. Until this is completed, there is a great deal of suffering. I would like to point out, though, that the suffering I am now speaking of is quite general and very indistinct. What you have here in the way of suffering is a painful awareness on your part that you are not yet established in your proper place with God.

What part does death play in the early stages of your Christian life? There is, first of all, a level of suffering which is caused by your hating and fearing the things that are bringing you to death. As that element of your human will begins to die, you will have less and less reaction to suffering and to the working of death in your life. It seems that we harden under the blows until, at last, there is a total end of all the natural elements of life. God pursues your natural life into all its hidden places. Your natural life, as corrupt as it is, will make any excuse and use even the holiest things as a refuge and hiding place. But God, in His mercy, comes to those places, seeking out your human will.

(A few people, having been pursued and followed into these last retreats, will finally abandon their hiding places. Alas, how few is this number, for none of us can really know or even imagine how strongly we cling to objects until at last they are taken away from us. The believer who thinks he is attached to nothing is actually bound by a thousand things unknown to himself.)

I mentioned that even after the total death of the will there is still some suffering. The soul is entirely rid of itself but has not yet been received into God. Something still exists. I do not know exactly what it is, a form, a human remnant that is still to vanish. But at last it does. I would say it is a tarnishing that is destroyed by a general indistinct suffering; an uneasiness which arises from being turned out of self without yet having been received into the great Original. The believer loses all possession of self—which is absolutely necessary if ever he is to be united with God; but only gradually does he know the new life of resurrection. (When I speak of the life of resurrection, I refer to that purely divine life—which dwells within each one of us—coming into full possession of the believer.)

When the very nature and will of your self have

died, when, in the experience of death, you fall into the embrace of God. . .when your inward parts are truly united to the Lord. . .with nothing between, then will you be united with the Lord.

Oddly, you yourself will not recognize this. Consequently, you cannot enjoy the fruits of this union— not until God brings this new life into being and you begin to realize that the Lord has become your vitalizing source.

A young bride who has fainted into the embrace of her husband is closely united with him, but she does not enjoy the blessedness of her union with him because she is unconscious. Nonetheless, her husband holds her in his arms while she is in a state of fainting that has come from excess love. He recalls her to life again tenderly by his caresses, and as she comes to consciousness she knows that she possesses him whom her soul loves *and* that she is possessed by him.

So, too, it is with the believer.

5

When you have been totally possessed by God, you will find that God is so perfectly Lord over your life that you can no longer do anything but what God pleases. That state goes on increasing. Your powerlessness is no longer painful now, but pleasant. Why? Because the very powerlessness is full of the life and power of the divine life. I mean by that, you are full of the divine will, i.e., all that God is, all that He thinks, all that He desires, and nothing else.

The inner man is in union with God when the life of the self-nature is vanished.

Nonetheless—and quite paradoxically—we cannot enjoy the fruits of this union until the moment of the soul's resurrection. At this time God causes the inner man to pass into Himself and gives you a pledge of assurance of a divine union—yes, even a divine marriage—between your inner man and the living God. The assurance and pledge of this union is so real that you can no longer have any doubt of it. The consummation is complete.

This union is so spiritual, so refined, so intimate, so much in divine life, that it is equally impossible to either imagine this union or to doubt it!

Do not think that such a thing as we discuss here can be imitated. This whole way of life is infinitely removed from any imagination. Such a resurrected believer is not even imaginative. He has nothing based on his own life, and is perfectly protected from being deceived by illusions. Everything takes place so deep within our interior that our imagination cannot reach it.

In previous chapters, we recounted your many passages through the way of faith. In the beginning of your Christian life, you are certain in your steps, the same as unbelievers are. Clarity is entirely opposite to faith. Through this passage that eventually leads to faith, you cannot enjoy any assurances at all. Everything you receive is something which has been revealed to you in a very general way. In fact, the foundation which the Lord laid down at the outset was one of a *general* sensing.

But now, as your soul experiences resurrection, everything becomes quite different. After your soul resurrects and becomes very advanced in God, there will be a marked change in your perspective. You may still not feel clear about anything, yet there *will be* a kind of clarity in you. It is a clarity given to you that is not for yourself, but rather, is there for the benefit of others.

Let me state that in another way. When you reach this stage, the Lord will give you illumination, but you will not be aware of it. The illumination will be certain only to the extent that it is simple and natural. I would like to emphasize again that this illumination is given for the benefit of others. (Please be aware that though this clarity is given for the benefit of others, the ones for whom it was intended will not always use it.)

When God, in your salvation, raises your spirit from the dead—that is, when He receives you into Himself and comes to dwell in you—at that time, there begins to appear a living germ within you. This germ of life begins to make itself apparent by coming from your inmost being and making its way to the outward. That little germ is—and has in it—the revealing of Jesus Christ.

> *When He was pleased to reveal His Son in me.*
> *(Gal. 1:15-16)*

This indwelling Lord has now begun to surface and to manifest Himself. He will live in you through the means of the loss of the Adam-life in you.

What am I saying here? I am saying that your resurrected inner man is received into God and—in God—your inner man is gradually changed and transformed by its union with Him. In the same way as food is transformed into the one who eats the food, so you will be transformed into the likeness of Him whom the inner man has passed into.

The wonder of all this is that this transformation takes place without the believer losing his distinct, individual existence.

When I speak of the beginnings of transformation, I speak of annihilation. Your form has been annihilated in order to take on His form. This is a continuing operation that goes on during your entire life, changing your soul more and more into the divine nature. This transformation deposits more and more of the divine quality into your deep inward parts. Your inner man is being changed. And what is it being changed into? Into an unchangeable and immovable state.

He makes us so fruitful in this way. But understand, you are fruitful *in Him*. I would not have you see yourself as being with the Lord and the fruit coming out of this touch with Him. No, I would have you to see the Lord transforming you until it is the Lord Himself who is the fruitfulness that comes forth.

After the Lord resurrects you, He makes you fruitful.

He brings others into your life. He brings someone to whom *He* wishes to commute divine love. You will express love to those people the Lord has given. This love that you will now be able to communicate will be far removed from natural feelings. (Divine love is infinitely stronger than the love of parents for their children.) The love you will now express to another is simply the movement of the resurrected life within you.

Your Lord does not deprive the senses and faculties of your soul forever to leave them dead. On the contrary, when the life of the spirit is communicated to the soul, this new life grows and increases degree by degree, enlivening all the powers and senses which have remained barren and unfruitful for so long. Your abilities and senses are made active by the life now working deep within. These abilities and senses will be activated in proportion to how much love has developed within your inner being. What we see, then, is the spirit—in your inmost portion—working actively through your mind, emotion and will. These activities of the soul are now really something coming out of the divine nature that dwells within you.

During the whole pilgrimage that I have discussed in the former chapters, the inmost part of the soul, in its journey through faith, has become less active . . . *until this last stage.* That changes in the stage of the resurrection of the soul. Now God wants to infuse your inner man with *divine* activity. Yet, as great as this sphere of activity might be, you will have an inner checking of your spirit when you seek to execute a self-oriented movement, for your inner man is under the control of the Lord who is dwelling deep therein.

6

Until now, I have spoken to you about stages, about degrees and about a pilgrimage. We have come now to the final state where there are no more such degrees. The state of glory is all that remains. The work of transformation, or at least the methods used to arrive at transformation, are now left behind. The future consists of, and enjoins, an infinite stretch of life; a life that grows more and more abundantly.

As God brings you to Himself, you are lost in God and are transformed; you receive the Lord's life plentifully. The love of God for a believer is beyond all our understanding. His loving pursuit of man is more than we can imagine. Some believers He pursues with not so much as an intermission. He seats Himself beside their door, attains them, and delights Himself in being with them at all times and in loading them with expressions of His love. He engraves this chaste, pure, and tender love upon that person's heart. John the

Beloved is such a man. He received this maternal affection from the Lord.

But for love to be as I have just described it, that love must be given by God in an advanced stage of being enveloped in divine life. In other words, this is a stage rather distant in the experience of grace. Be assured, then, that such an encounter of love is neither of the emotions nor of the natural man.

The stages of this pilgrimage which bring you toward faith are each characterized by prayer that is an ever- ascending movement toward silence. That is, the powers of the self-nature gradually become totally quieted. The final stages of prayer are a complete secession of every tiny effort. When you have arrived at this point in your pilgrimage, you will actually come to a place where you cannot lay hold of any prayer at all. The ability to pray has been taken away. You cannot even set aside certain times for prayer.

You will be, therefore, led to think that you have absolutely lost every kind of devotion to the Lord. This is the final stage. You will have come to that place where you have nothing at all but *naked faith*.

But what about when life returns after death? Does prayer return? Yes, prayer returns when life returns. And what are the characteristics of prayer in this new dimension? Prayer is accompanied by a marvelous ease. With this prayer comes a devotion which is sweet, gentle and very much in spirit; it is prayer that is always in God.

Formerly, your devotion caused you to sink within yourself that you might enjoy God. But the devotion that comes after the resurrection of your soul will draw you out of yourself. The purpose of devotion is no longer that of enjoying God. The purpose of devotion now will be that you may be more and more lost in God and changed into Him.

The difference in these two types of prayer is a very remarkable one. When the soul is in the state of death it is silent. The silence is known by God alone. There is no silence in any other part of your being. The stillness is barren and accompanied by frantic rambling. There is no mark of silence except the impossibility of addressing God either with lips or heart. After the resurrection, the soul is silent, yet this silence is accompanied by a great deal of fruitfulness. Furthermore, prayer is accompanied by an exceedingly pure and refined anointing which is deliciously diffused over the senses. This enjoyment is so pure that it does not cause any hindrances to advancement; rather, it progresses into the divine light. There are no stains left in this enjoyment.

If you reach the level to which I now refer, it will be impossible for you to take what does not belong to you. Instead, you receive with passive willingness whatever impressions are made upon you from a source that is coming from deep within.

As to suffering, if you reach this advanced level of life, I could venture to say you would be free from suffering, no matter what your circumstances, *except* for the fact that God finds it necessary that such an advanced saint suffer for the sake of others not so advanced. If God could cause the younger Christian to correspond to the older one, then the older one would need not suffer. But the stage of development that the younger Christian is in is one which he cannot bear. Therefore, it becomes necessary for the older believer to suffer in order for the younger one to receive what God wants him to have. What God wants to give the younger believer is communicated to him through the suffering of the older and more advanced believer.

Nor is it proper for the younger Christian to say, *I do not want to allow this older one to suffer for me.* The Lord is anxious that this younger saint die to a certain strength of self within. . .even that strength which causes him to say, *I desire only God, and do not wish to see others suffer.* If the younger Christian were to reject the suffering of the older Christian, the younger one would withdraw himself from God's order and would arrest his own personal progress. This vicarious, substitutionary suffering of the older saint for the younger is only a means to reach a certain end. The older believer's suffering will finally disappear when the means have accomplished their end.

This suffering, besides being a means of communicating something of God to the younger believer, also causes the production of grace and strength in the spirit of that younger one. When the sufferings are completed, when they have finished their purpose, when God does not need to use them anymore as a means to communicate Himself or His will through the sufferings, then He withdraws the sufferings and He communicates Himself directly to the younger Christian. At the time when the sufferings disappear, the older believer fully realizes the purpose of his suffering. When that time comes . . .when he *knows* what he has been suffering for in God's purpose, he will actually become attached to his sufferings, will anchor himself in his sufferings, and will find himself one with those sufferings. . .in God.

But God cannot allow such a one to have both this knowledge *and* also continue to have the suffering; therefore, He removes the suffering. What state does the believer then find himself in? He is just as before;

dead to all suffering and continuing in close union with God.

I come back, then, to what I said a moment ago: In the resurrected state, there comes an utter silence of the inner man. By that silence, this advanced believer lives in God and lives from God. It is in this silent state that he communicates with God. *Silence* becomes both a wonderful *transmission* and *receiving* of divine communication.

What are we seeing here? The inner man has become a partaker of an unutterable, inexpressible communion that goes on with the Trinity. The Father of Spirits imparts His spiritual fertility and makes the inner man to be one with the Lord Himself. Just as the believer's spirit has always been one with the divine spirit ever since his conversion, now his inner man is united with the Lord by means of having been transformed. In this state, one believer's inner man can fellowship with the inner man of another believer, in silence, provided both are sufficiently pure.

It is also here that unutterable secrets are revealed, not by illumination, which is momentary, but revealed in God Himself. (It is in God that all secrets are hidden.)

We are speaking of a resurrected soul and its capacity to perceive.

You might think that when you reached this point

you would have great clarity. Yet, when you reach this point, you will find that you still do not see clearly. At least from *your* viewpoint you will not see clearly. (The clarity will be known by those with whom you communicate.)

When you reach this advanced stage, whatever you say will be said very naturally; not as though you were saying something worthy of attention. The advanced soul sees nothing special in what he is saying. Ah, but the ones hearing may consider the words to be quite extraordinary. The hearers probably will not have ever experienced what the inward spirit is speaking about. Therefore, the one speaking may expect one of two reactions from his hearers:

The one hearing may feel that what he has heard is very clear and very wonderful. Or, he may just as likely decide that he has heard something fanatical. . .after all, he has never experienced what is being said. Even in this latter case, there is the possibility the hearer knows what he has heard is reality, despite the fact that he does not know it in experience.

When you are still dwelling among the gifts, you have distinct—but only momentary—illuminations. The more advanced you become, the less definite will be your illuminations. If you reach the level described here, you will have *only* a *general* illumination. That illumination is of God Himself, nothing more. You will not have any specific illuminations.

From out of this very general light, which is God Himself, you will draw whatever you need. Part of what you receive may go through you to others. They, in turn, may receive certain aspects of this light (which is out of God) because they sense a need within themselves for guidance.

7

At this point there are many things we could consider concerning a believer whose inner being has been transformed to the point that he is full of God's life. There is so much. . .a thousand things. . .that God dearly cherishes for Himself in these matters. But He is also a jealous God. Many of these lovely things He covers with an outer covering that looks very ordinary, even abased. I am saying to you that God sometimes takes His most beloved saints and seems to degrade them; nonetheless, it would require a volume to write all the things He loves about these seemingly common ones.

Should you reach this final level of which I have heretofore spoken, you will live in God, and that without interruption, just as a fish lives in the sea and is never out of that sea for even a moment. There you will be in inexpressible happiness even though you may be loaded down with many sufferings which God has laid upon you for the benefit of others.

Should you come to this level of transformation—and even advance beyond this level—you will become so simple that you will live perpetually without even a thought for yourself. . .and surprisingly, without a thought for others. You will have but one objective: to do the will of God. Therein lies the source of much of the suffering that will come to you. You will want to do the will of God without any thought of self *and* without any thought of others. Nonetheless, you have to live with and deal with others. You will be living with those who have not come to such a deep level, and these believers will try to compel you to care for yourself and to take precautions, etc. It is this which will cause the more advanced Christian a great deal of suffering: others seeking to compel him to do something which he simply cannot do. In other words, others cause him suffering simply because they are not able to align themselves with the will of God.

If you come to this point in your pilgrimage to the center of God, your cross will be most severe. God will keep you under the most abject humiliation; that, despite the fact that the Lord will find great delight in your inner man. The Lord will cause you to appear very feeble and very ordinary.

It is at this point that you can receive within yourself all the experience of Jesus Christ.

Having come thus far in your pilgrimage into God, you will be clothed upon by *His* disposition and *His* inclinations; but do not forget you will also be clothed upon by *His* sufferings. Then—and only then—will you understand what man has cost Him and what all our faithlessness toward Him has done to Him. Then you will be able to comprehend what the redemption of Jesus Christ really is and how He births His children.

The level that I am speaking of, then, is one of complete inner transformation. It can be recognized by the fact that there is little or no distinction between the Lord and the internal soul which He has overcome. The Lord has moved outward, out of the human spirit and gradually reached forth until the soul has become like unto the spirit. The soul is no longer able to separate itself from God. It seems that everything now is God. Why? Because the inner man has passed into its original source. It has reunited itself with the *All*.

I am giving you here only a general sketch, an outline, of what it is that may await you in your future journey. Experience with the Lord will teach you the rest.

Is it possible that a believer can be transformed into an even more perfect state than has been described here?

If that were possible, then the believer would find himself actually partaking of God's very infinity. He would find an extended quality within himself with everything expanded. He would often find the whole earth appearing to be a little point in comparison with the wonderful breadth and extension which he has experienced. Whatever he would find in the will of God would expand his soul (or his regenerated spirit—as human spirit and human soul have now become almost one and the same). And if that expanding were to continue, the soul would pass out entirely. To restrain this and to prevent it from happening, the soul is contracted by things around it that are not in the will of God!

I would point out to you that it is your spirit which is the means for bringing about transformation. The center of your being is nothing other than all your faculties united to your spirit. . .including your very will. The more you are transformed, the more your spirit—and your will in that spirit—is changed and passed into that which is of God. The soul acts and works within the divine spirit. Therefore, the will of the divine spirit is substituted for your will. This is such a natural thing that you will not be able to tell whether your own will is doing the will of God or the will of God is becoming your will.

The Lord frequently extracts quite unusual sacrifices from saints who are so transformed; yet, I must add that there really is no cost involved, for such a love will sacrifice everything to Him, and that without thought or hesitation. In fact, it is the smaller sacrifices which cost the most. The greater ones cost the least, for they are not required until the soul is in a condition to acquiesce to them without difficulty.

This is what is said of Jesus Christ on His coming into the world:

> Then I said, "Behold, I come; in the scroll of the book it is written of me; I delight to do Thy will, O my God; Thy Law is within my heart."
>
> *Psalm 11:7-8*

Be assured that when the Lord Christ comes into any believer, He becomes the living principle of that person. When He has finished His work in that one, He becomes the eternal priest who unceasingly fulfills His priestly office within that person's inner man. This is a sublime thing and continues until the believer is carried to glory.

When your inner man has been transformed, you will be destined by the Lord for giving assistance to others in a most tangible way. You will no longer be anxious about anything, especially about yourself, for you have nothing to lose. Consequently, God can then use you to bring others into the very same path of this Spirit-directed life. While you are still self-possessed, you cannot possibly be used of the Lord for this purpose. Why? Because you do not yet follow the will of the Lord utterly. You invariably mix the Lord's will with your own reasoning and pseudo-wisdom. You would always be withholding something from those whom you were guiding and leading.

I am not saying a transformed person will always point out someone else's shortcomings. Not at all. I would say that the Lord does not permit a mature Christian to point out to another Christian what he sees as a hindrance in the other's life . . . *and* what must come to pass in that life. To share so much would damage the other person's progress. No, the truly transformed one will speak in general terms and in general principles, and if the transformed one does say things that are hard, then you must remember Christ even had the ability to speak harshly. But also remember that your Lord has the ability to bestow upon proper heirs a secret strength to bear what is heard.

At the very least, I would say our Lord gives a secret strength to the ones whom He has chosen solely for Himself. This impartation of His strength to the one upon whom He is working—so that He might bring that one to complete transformation—ah, that is the touchstone of the whole matter.

Union With God ————————

The Poems of
Jeanne Guyon

Virtually nothing is known about the circumstances, the time or the location of the writing of the poems of Jeanne Guyon. Consequently these poems are difficult to categorize. We have chosen, therefore, to arrange them by beginning with her earliest known poem which was written at the age of nineteen. This is a poem which proved incredibly prophetic of her entire life. The closing poems carry in them the theme of imprisonment. Which of these poems were actually written during her nine years of prison life and which ones were written later, during the period of her banishment, we do not know.

Union With God ———————

WRITTEN AT AGE NINETEEN

By sufferings only can we know
The nature of the life we live:
The trial of our souls, they show,
How true, how pure, the love we give.
To leave my love in doubt would be
No less disgrace than misery.

I welcome, then, with heart sincere,
The cross my Savior bids me take:
No load, no trial is severe,
That's borne or suffered for His sake:
And thus my sorrows shall proclaim
A love that's worthy of the name.

DIVINE JUSTICE

Thou hast no lightnings, O thou Just!
Or I their force should know;
And, if thou strike me into dust,
My soul approves the blow.

The heart that values less its ease,
Than it adores thy ways,
In thine avenging anger sees
A subject of its praise.

Pleased I could lie, conceal'd and lost,
In shades of central night;
Not to avoid thy wrath, thou know'st,
But lest I grieve thy sight.

Smite me, O thou whom I provoke!
And I will love thee still.
The well-deserved and righteous stroke
Shall please me, though it kill.

Am I not worthy to sustain
The worst thou canst devise?
And dare I seek thy throne again,
And meet thy sacred eyes?

Far from afflicting, thou art kind,
And in my saddest hours,
An unction of thy grace I find
Pervading all my powers.

Alas! Thou *spar'st* me yet again,
And when thy wrath should move,
Too gentle to endure my pain
Thou sooth'st me with thy love.

I have no punishment to fear;
But, ah! That smile from thee
Imparts a pang far more severe
Than woe itself would be.

THE DEALINGS OF GOD

'Twas my purpose, on a day,
To embark and sail away.
As I climb'd the vessel's side,
Love was sporting in the tide;
"Come," He said, "ascend make haste,
Launch into the boundless waste."

Many mariners were there,
Having each his separate care;
They, that row'd us, held their eyes
Fix'd upon the starry skies;
Others steer'd or turn'd the sails
To receive the shifting gales.

Love, with power Divine supplied,
Suddenly my courage tried;
In a moment it was night,
Ship and skies were out of sight;'
On the briny wave I lay,
Floating rushes all my stay.

Did I with resentment burn
At this unexpected turn?
Did I wish myself on shore,
Never to forsake it more?
No— *"My soul,"* I cried, *"be still;*
If I must be lost, I will."

Next He hasten'd to convey
Both my frail supports away;
Seized my rushes; bade the waves
Yawn into a thousand graves.
Down I went, and sank as lead,
Ocean closing o'er my head.

Still, however, life was safe;
And I saw Him turn and laugh;
"Friend," He cried, "adieu! Lie low,
While the wintry storms shall blow;
When the spring has calm'd the main,
You shall rise, and float again."

Soon I saw Him with dismay
Spread His plumes, and soar away,
Now I mark His rapid flight;
Now He leaves my aching sight
He is gone whom I adore,
'Tis in vain to seek Him more.

How I trembled then and fear'd,
When my Love had disappear'd!
"Wilt thou leave me thus," I cried,
"Whelm'd beneath the rolling tide?"
Vain attempt to reach His ear!
Love was gone, and would not hear.

Union With God

Ah! Return and love me still;
See me subject to thy will;
Frown with wrath, or smile with grace
Only let me see thy face!
Evil I have none to fear;
All is good, if Thou art near.

Yet He leaves me, cruel fate!
Leaves me in my lost estate;
Have I sinn'd? Oh, say wherein?
Tell me, and forgive my sin!
King, and Lord, whom I adore,
Shall I see thy face no more?

Be not angry I resign
Henceforth all my will to thine.
I consent that Thou depart,
Though thine absence breaks my heart
Go then, and for ever, too;
All is right that Thou wilt do.

This was just what Love intended;
He was now no more offended;
Soon as I became a child,
Love return'd to me and smiled.
Never strife shall more betide
'Twixt the Bridegroom and His bride.

THE JOY OF THE CROSS

Long plunged in sorrow, I resign
My soul to that dear hand of thine,
Without reserve or fear:
That hand shall wipe my streaming eyes;
Or into smiles of glad surprise
Transform the falling tear.

My soul possession is thy love;
In earth beneath, or heaven above,
I have no other store;
And though with fervent suit I pray,
And importune thee, night and day,
I ask thee nothing more.

My rapid hours pursue the course,
Prescribed them by love's sweetest force
And by thy sovereign will,
Without a wish to escape my doom;
Though still a sufferer from the womb,
And doom'd to suffer still.

By thy command, where'er I stray,
Sorrow attends me all my way,
A never failing friend,
And, if my sufferings may augment
Thy praise, behold me well content,
Let *Sorrow* still attend!

Adieu! Ye vain delights of earth,
Insipid sports, and childish mirth,
I taste no sweets in you;
Unknown delights are in the cross,
All joy beside to me is dross;
And Jesus thought so too.

The *Cross!* O ravishment and bliss—
How grateful e'en its anguish is;
Its bitterness how sweet!
There every sense, and all the mind,
In all her faculties refined,
Taste happiness complete.

Souls, once enabled to disdain
Base, sublunary joys, maintain
Their dignity secure;
The fever of desire is pass'd,
And Love has all its genuine taste,
Is delicate and pure.

Self-love no grace in Sorrow sees,
Consults her own peculiar ease:
'Tis all the bliss she knows;
But nobler aims true Love employ,
In self-denial is her joy,
In suffering her repose.

Sorrow and Love go side by side;
Nor height nor depth can e'er divide
Their heaven-appointed bands;
Those dear associates still are one,
Nor, till the race of life is run,
Disjoin their wedded hands.

Jesus, avenger of our fall,
Thou faithful lover, above all
The cross have ever borne!
O tell me life is in thy voice
How much afflictions were thy choice,
And sloth and easy thy scorn!

Thy choice and mine shall be the same,
Inspirer of that holy flame
Which must for ever blaze!
To take the cross and follow thee,
Where love and duty lead, shall be
My portion and my praise.

MY COUNTRY, LORD, ART THOU ALONE

O thou by long experience tried,
Near whom no grief can long abide;
My Lord! How full of sweet content,
I pass my years of banishment.

All scenes alike engaging prove
To souls impress'd with sacred love;
Where'er they dwell, they dwell in Thee,
In heaven, in earth, or on the sea.

To me remains nor place nor time;
My country is in every clime;
I can be calm and free from care
On any shore, since God is there.

While place we seek, or place we shun,
The soul finds happiness in none:
But with a God to guide our way,
'Tis equal joy to go or stay.

Could I be cast where Thou art not,
That were indeed a dreadful lot;
But regions none remote I call,
Secure of finding God in all.

My country, Lord, art Thou alone:
No other can I claim or own;
The point where all my wishes meet,
My law, my love; life's only sweet.

I hold by nothing here below;
Appoint my journey, and I go;
Though pierced by scorn, oppressed by pride,
I feel the good, feel nought beside.

No frowns of men can hurtful prove
To souls on fire with heavenly love;
Though men and devils both condemn,
No gloomy days arise for them.

Ah, then! to His embrace repair,
My soul, —thou art no stranger there;
There love Divine shall be thy guard,
And peace and safety thy reward.

THE UNLOVED LOVER

My heart is easy, and my burden light;
I smile, though sad, when God is in my sight.
The more my woes in secret I deplore,
I taste thy goodness, and I love thee more.

There, while a solemn stillness reigns around,
Faith, love, and hope, within my soul abound;
And while the world suppose me lost in care,
The joys of angels unperceived I share.

Thy creatures wrong thee, O thou Sovereign Good!
Thou art not loved, because not understood,
This grieves me most, that vain pursuits beguile
Ungrateful men, regardless of thy smile.

Frail beauty and false honor are adored;
While Thee they scorn, and trifle with thy word;
Pass, unconcern'd, a Savior's sorrows by,
And hunt their ruin with a zeal to die.

Awaiting

"Father adored! Thy holy will be done;
 Low at thy feet I lie,
Thy loving chastisement I would not shun,
 Nor from thine anger fly.
My heart is weak, but wean'd from all beside,
And to thy will resign'd whate'er betide"

HASTEN

Ah, reign wherever man is found,
My Spouse, beloved and Divine!
Then I am rich, and then abound,
When every human heart is thine.

A thousand sorrows pierce my soul,
To think that all are not thine own;
Ah, be adored from pole to pole;—
Where is thy zeal? *Arise Be known.*

A Little Bird I Am

A little bird I am,
Shut from the fields of air;
And in my cage I sit and sing
To Him who placed me there;
Well pleased a prisoner to be,
Because, my God, it pleases Thee.

Nought have I else to do;
I sing the whole day long;
And He whom most I love to please,
Doth listen to my song;
He caught and bound my wandering wing,
But still He bends to hear me sing.

Thou hast an ear to hear;
A heart to love and bless;
And, though my notes were e'er so rude,
Thou wouldst not hear the less;
Because thou knowest, as they fall,
That Love, sweet Love, inspires them all.

My Cage confines me round;
Abroad I cannot fly;
But though my wing is closely bound,
My heart's at liberty.
My prison walls can not control
The flight, the freedom of the soul.

Oh! It is good to soar
These bolts and bars above,
To Him whose purpose I adore,
Whose providence I love;
And in thy mighty will to find
The joy, the freedom of the mind.

LOVE CONSTITUTES MY CRIME

Love constitutes my crime;
For this they keep me here,
Imprison'd thus so long a time
For Him I hold so dear;
And yet I am, as when I came,
The subject of this holy flame.

How can I better grow!
How from my own heart fly!
Those who imprison me should know
True love can never die.
Yea, tread and crush it with disdain,
And it will live and burn again.

And am I then to blame?
He's always in my sight;
And having once inspired the flame,
He always keeps it bright.
For this they smite me and reprove,
Because I cannot cease to love.

What power shall dim its ray,
Dropped burning from above!
Eternal life shall ne'er decay;
God is the life of love.
And when its source of life is o'er,
And only then, 'twill shine no more.

GOD'S GLORY AND GOODNESS

Infinite God! My great, unrivall'd One!
Whose light eclipses that of yonder sun;
Compared with thine, how dim its beauty seems
How quench'd the radiance of its golden beams!

O God! Your creatures, in one strain, agree;—
All, in all times and places, speak of thee
Even I, with trembling heart and stammering tongue
Attempt thy praise, and join the general song

Almighty Former of this wondrous plan
Faintly reflected in thine image, man;
Holy and just! The greatness of whose name
Fills and supports this universal frame!—

Diffused throughout infinitude of space,
Who are thyself thine own vast dwelling-place
Soul of our soul! Whom yet no sense of ours
Discerns, eluding our most active powers;

Encircling shades attend thine awful throne;
That veil thy face, and keep thee still unknown.
Unknown, though dwelling in our inmost part,
Lord of the thoughts, and sovereign of the heart—

Thou art my bliss! The light by which I move!
In thee, O God! Dwells all that I can love.
Where'er I turn, I see thy power and grace,
Which ever watch and bless our heedless race.

Oh! Then, repeat the truth, that never tires;
No God is like the God my soul desires;
He, at whose voice heaven trembles, even He,
Great as He is, knows how to stoop to me.

Vain pageantry and pomp of earth, adieu!
Have no wish, no memory for you!
Rich in God's love, I feel my noblest pride
Spring from the sense of having nought beside.

GOD THE FOUNTAIN OF LOVE TO HIS CHILDREN

I Love Thee, Lord, but with no love of mine,
For I have none to give;
I love thee, Lord; but all the love is thine.
For by thy love I love.
I am as nothing, and rejoice to be
Emptied, and lost, and swallow'd up in thee

Thou, Lord, alone, art all thy children need,
And there is none beside;
From thee the streams of blessedness proceed;
In thee the bless'd abide.
Fountain of life, and all-abounding grace,
Our source, our centre, and our dwelling place.

THE ACQUIESCENCE OF PURE LOVE

Love! If thy destined sacrifice am I,
Come, slay thy victim, and prepare thy fires;
Plunged in thy depths of mercy, let me die
The death which every soul that lives, desires.

I watch my hours, and see them fleet away;
The time is long that I have languish'd here
Yet all my thoughts thy purposes obey,
With no reluctance, cheerful and sincere.

To me 'tis equal, whether love ordain
My life or death, appoint me pain or ease,
My soul perceives no real ill in pain
In ease or health no real good she sees.

One good she covets, and that good alone—
To choose thy will, from selfish bias free;
And to prefer a cottage to a throne,
And grief to comfort, if it pleases thee.

That we should bear the cross is thy command.
Die to the world, and live to self no more;
Suffer, unmoved, beneath the rudest hand;
When shipwreck'd pleased, as when upon the shore.

PRISONS DO NOT EXCLUDE GOD

Strong are the walls around me,
That hold me all the day;
But they who thus have bound me,
Cannot keep God away;
My very dungeon walls are dear,
Because the God I love is here.

They know, who thus oppress me,
'Tis hard to be alone;
But know not, One can bless me,
Who comes through bars and stone:
He makes my dungeon's darkness bright,
And fills my bosom with delight.

Thy Love, O God, restores me
From sighs and tears to praise;
And deep my soul adores thee,
Nor thinks of time or place:
I ask no more, in good or ill,
But union with thy holy will.

'Tis that which makes my treasure,
'Tis that which brings my gain;
Converting woe to pleasure,
And reaping joy from pain.
Oh, 'tis enough, whate'er befall,
To know that God is All In All.

GOD KNOWN BY LOVING HIM

'Tis not the skill of human art,
Which gives me power my God to know;
The sacred lessons of the heart
Come not from instruments below.

Love is my teacher. He can tell
The wonders that He learnt above:
No other master knows so well;—
This Love alone can tell of Love.

Oh! Then, of God if thou wouldst learn,
His wisdom, goodness, glory see;
All human arts and knowledge spurn,
Let Love alone thy teacher be.

Love is my master. When it breaks,
The morning light, with rising ray,
To thee, O God! My spirit wakes,
And Love instructs it all the day.

And when the gleams of day retire,
And midnight spreads its dark control,
Love's secret whispers still inspire
Their holy lessons in the soul.

THOUGHTS OF GOD IN THE NIGHT

O Night! Propitious to my views,
Thy sable awning wide diffuse!
Conceal alike my joy and pain,
Nor draw thy curtain back again,
Though morning, by the tears she shows,
Seems to participate my woes.

Ye stars! Whose faint and feeble fires
Express my languishing desires,
Whose slender beams pervade the skies
As silent as my secret sighs,
Those emanations of a soul
That darts her fires beyond the pole;—

Your rays, that scarce assist the sight,
That pierce, but not displace the night,
That shine, indeed, but nothing show
Of all those various scenes below,
Bring no disturbance, rather prove
Incentives to a sacred love.

Thou moon! Whose never-failing course
Bespeaks a providential force,
Go, tell the tidings of my flame
To Him who calls the stars by name;
Whose absence kills, whose presence cheers,
Who blots or brightens all my years.

While, in the blue abyss of space,
Thine orb performs its rapid race;
Still whisper in His listening ears
The language of my sighs and tears;
Tell Him, I seek Him far below,
Lost in a wilderness of woe.

Ye thought-composing, silent hours,
Diffusing peace o'er all my powers;
Friends of the pensive! Who conceal,
In darkest shades, the flames I feel;
To you I trust, and safely may,
The love that wastes my strength away.

How calm, amid the night, my mind!
How perfect is the peace I find!
Oh! Hush, be still, my every part,
My tongue, my pulse, my beating heart!
That love, aspiring to its cause,
May suffer not a moment's pause.

Omniscient God, whose notice deigns
To try the heart and search the reins,
Compassionate the numerous woes
I dare to thee alone disclose,
Oh! Save me from the cruel hands
Of men who fear not thy commands.

Love, all-subduing and Divine,
Care for a creature truly thine;
Reign in a heart disposed to own
No sovereign but thyself alone;
Cherish a bride who cannot rove,
Nor quit thee for a meaner love.

THE ENTIRE SURRENDER

Peace has unveil'd her smiling face,
And woos thy soul to her embrace;
Enjoy'd with ease, if thou refrain
From selfish love, else sought in vain;
She dwells with all who truth prefer,
But seeks not them who seek not her.

Yield to the Lord with simple heart,
All that thou hast, and all thou art;
Renounce all strength but strength Divine,
And peace shall be for ever thine;
Behold the path which I have trod—
My path till I go home to God.

GLORY TO GOD ALONE

O Loved! But not enough, though dearer far
Than self and its most loved enjoyments are;
None duly loves thee, but who, nobly free
From sensual objects, finds his All in thee.

Glory of God! thou stranger here below,
Whom man nor knows, nor feels a wish to know,
Our faith and reason are both shock'd to find
Man in the post of honour, thee behind.

My soul! Rest happy in thy low estate,
Nor hope nor wish to be esteem'd or great:
To take the impression of a Will Divine,
Be that thy glory, and those riches thine.

Confess Him righteous in His just decrees,
Love what He loves, and let His pleasures please;
Die Daily; from the touch of sin recede;
Then thou hast crown'd Him, and He reigns indeed.

The Light Above Us

There is light in yonder skies,
A light unseen by outward eyes;—
But clear and bright to inward sense,
It shines, the star of Providence.

The radiance of the central throne,
It comes from God, and God alone;
The ray that never yet grew pale.
The star that shines within the veil."

And faith, uncheck'd by earthly fears,
Shall life its eye, though fill'd with tears,
And while around 'tis dark as night,
Untired, shall mark that heavenly light.

In vain they smite me. Men but do
What God permits with different view;—
To outward sight they wield the rod,
But faith proclaims it all of God.

Unmoved, then, let me keep my way,
Supported by that cheering ray,
Which, shining distant, renders clear
The clouds and darkness thronging near.

TRUTH AND DIVINE LOVE REJECTED BY THE WORLD

O Love, of pure and heavenly birth!
O simple Truth, scarce known on earth!
Whom men resist with stubborn will;—
And, more perverse and daring still,
Smother and quench with reasonings vain,
While error and deception reign.

Whence comes it that, your power the same
As His on high from whom you came,
Ye rarely find a listening ear,
Or heart that makes you welcome here?—
Because ye bring reproach and pain,
Where'er ye visit, in your train.

The world is proud, and cannot bear
The scorn and calumny ye share;—
The praise of men, the mark *they* mean,
They fly the place where ye are seen.
Pure Love, with scandal in the rear,
Suits not the vain: it costs too dear.

Then let the price be what it may,
Though poor, I am prepared to pay;—
Come shame, come sorrow; spite of tears,
Weakness, and heart-oppressing fears,
One soul, at least, shall not repine
To give *you* room: come, reign in mine!

THE TESTIMONY OF DIVINE ADOPTION

How happy are the new-born race,
Partakers of *adopting grace!*
How pure the bliss they share
Hid from the world and all its eyes,
Within their heart the blessing lies,
And conscience feels it there.

The moment we Believe, 'tis ours:
And if we love with *all our powers*
The God from whom it came,
And if we serve with hearts sincere,
'Tis still discernible and clear,
An undisputed claim.

But ah! If *foul and willful sin*
Stain and dishonour us within,
Farewell the joy we knew;
Again the salves of Nature's sway,
In lab'rinths of our own we stray,
Without a guide or clue.

The chaste and pure, who fear to grieve
The gracious Spirit they receive,
His work distinctly trace;
And strong in undissembling love,
Boldly assert, and clearly prove,
Their hearts His dwelling-place.

O messenger of dear delight!
Whose voice dispels the deepest night,
Sweet, peace-proclaiming Dove!
With thee at hand to soothe our pains,
No wish unsatisfied remains,
No task but that of Love.

'Tis Love unites what Sin divides:
The centre where all bliss resides
To which the soul once brought,
Reclining on the first great Cause,
From His abounding sweetness draws
Peace, passing human thought.

Sorrow foregoes its nature there,
And life assumes a tranquil air,
Divested of its woes;
There, sovereign goodness soothes the breast,
Till then, incapable of rest,
In sacred sure repose.

Union With God

THE CHRONICLES OF HEAVEN *(Edwards)*

Christ Before Creation 8.99
The Beginning 8.99
The Escape 8.99
The Birth 8.99
The Triumph 8.99
The Return 8.99

THE COLLECTED WORKS OF T. AUSTIN-SPARKS

The Centrality of Jesus Christ 19.95
The House of God 29.95
Ministry 29.95
Service 19.95
Spiritual Foundations 29.95
The Things of the Spirit 10.95
Prayer 14.95
The On-High Calling 10.95
Rivers of Living Water 8.95
The Power of His Resurrection 8.95

COMFORT AND HEALING

A Tale of Three Kings *(Edwards)* 8.99
The Prisoner in the Third Cell *(Edwards)* 9.99
Letters to a Devastated Christian *(Edwards)* 7.95
Exquisite Agony *(Edwards)* 9.95
Dear Lillian *(Edwards) paperback* 5.95
Dear Lillian *(Edwards) hardcover* 9.99

OTHER BOOKS ON CHURCH LIFE

Climb the Highest Mountain *(Edwards)* 12.95
The Torch of the Testimony *(Kennedy)* 14.95
The Passing of the Torch *(Chen)* 9.95
Going to Church in the First Century *(Banks)* 5.95
When the Church was Young *(Loosley)* 8.95
Church Unity *(Litzman,Nee,Edwards)* 10.95
Let's Return to Christian Unity *(Kurosaki)* 10.95

CHRISTIAN LIVING

The Christian Woman . . . Set Free *(Edwards)* 12.95
Your Lord Is a Blue Collar Worker *(Edwards)* 7.95
The Autobiography of Jeanne Guyon 19.95
Final Steps in Christian Maturity *(Guyon)* 12.95
Turkeys and Eagles *(Lord)* 9.95
The Life of Jeanne Guyon *(T.C. Upham)* 17.95
Life's Ultimate Privilege *(Fromke)* 10.00
Unto Full Stature *(Fromke)* 10.00
All and Only *(Kilpatrick)* 8.95
Adoration *(Kilpatrick)* 9.95
Release of the Spirit *(Nee)* 9.99
Bone of His Bone *(Huegel) modernized* 9.95
You Can Witness with Confidence *(Rinker)* 10.95

Union With God ─────────────

———————————————Union With God

Union With God ——————

CPSIA information can be obtained
at www.ICGtesting.com
Printed in the USA
LVHW090741280220
648388LV00005B/128